Nadim was being naughty. He brought a plastic scorpion to school.

"Look at my creepy-crawly," he said.

The scorpion had big claws.
"Its sting is awesome," said Nadim.

"Mrs May is a good sport," said Chip. "Let's put the scorpion on the floor and call her."

"Mrs May," called Craig, "there's a creepy-crawly on the floor. It came in the door."

"It looks like a scorpion," said Nadim.

"Look at this poor scorpion," said Mrs May. "Its claw is missing."

"I'll keep it in my bag for today," said Mrs May. "It's time for you all to settle down."

At morning break, Craig got out his Top Score cards. He had a new game called War Force.

Craig gave out all the cards. “The card with the top score wins,” said Craig.

Corex the Gaul was on Craig's card.

Nadim had Hawk the Norman.

Chip had Augan the Roman.

Wilf had Thorkel the Viking.

"Look, Thorkel has horns on his helmet," said Wilf. "Vikings didn't have horned helmets."

"I thought they fought with axes," said Chip. Just then, Mrs May saw the boys.

“What a morning,” she said. “I think the cards can go in my bag, with the scorpion.”

"Find out about the Vikings. You can all give a little talk to the class."

Craig looked up Viking helmets. "You were right," he said. "They didn't have horns on them."

"What's more," said Nadim, "they had swords and they had axes. I'm not sure if they had horses."

"Here is a Norse story," said Craig.
"Thor was the Viking god of thunder."

“I’ll draw a Viking hut,” said Chip.
“This hut has straw on the roof.”

Chip did drawings of Viking huts.

Craig recorded a Norse story.

Nadim made a Viking ship.

Wilf drew what Vikings wore.

The boys put a display on the wall. They gave a talk in the hall.

They had lots of applause.

“You four boys did well, in the end,” said Mrs May.